Wednesday Mourning:

A Theology of Grief

N.J. Bennett

Illustrated by
Bronwyn Bennett Lane
Wynnsical Works

Produced by
Megan Bennett

Bennett Hall Projects
Copyright © 1986

Revised © 2018

ISBN: 978-1500495510

To my daughters, Meg and Wynn, who were born from my heart, not from my womb. And to my husband, Roy, who has journeyed beside me…always beside me.

Table of Contents

Wednesday Mourning: A Theology of Grief
"Wednesday's child is full of woe..."

"Don't you believe that there is
in man a deep so profound
as to be hidden even to him in whom it is?"
St. Augustine

History has shown us both through its art and its literature that suffering is common to man. Although it has been and continues to be a common journey, it is unrelentingly individual.

Grief is like being blindfolded and forced to walk the plank. You walk, with a knife pressing through your backbone, pricking your heart. You are dizzy in your darkness, faltering with every step until the quivering, narrow plank is no more; and you fall... whirling into space not caring you live or die... preferring death to ease your pain.

Yet in that empty, midnight, solitary space there is a healing hand that intercepts your fall and gently places you on solid ground, and then hides you in the hollow of that same hand. He is the Great I Am, the Healer, the Lover of our souls, the Maker of our hearts.

We have a choice to make. When we are tossed into grief's maelstrom, do we cling to the hand of a Sovereign God? Or do we despise it and consequently drown in the bitter, dark, fathomless waters into which grief will surely plummet us?

Griever, let sorrow be your companion; let its unyielding arms embrace you. Open up the clenched fist that only wants to know 'why?' and cling to the hand that wants to show you 'how'. You will never be the same.

There is a small, flat, slab of cement lying in a common graveyard in Western Canada. It is covered by snow most of the year. It is left alone. No one tends it. Its lovers live thousands of miles away. The inscription simply reads:

Levi Nielsen Bennett
Born into the presence of God
December 3, 1986

Under that simple tombstone lies the body of our baby son who died in my womb eleven days before his fullterm birth. This, I am told, is called *stillbirth*. Yes, he was still. His little blue eyes couldn't see my tears. He was still. His perfect little fingers couldn't grasp mine. His little heart was still; and so was mine.

Now, many years later I share my journal with you. It is my desire that you will find hope. Not hope in *hope*, but hope in *God*, who gives grace upon grace, upon grace, upon grace... I pray you will find hope in His Word, and know for certain that His promises are true. I pray that you will trust Him, know His character (who He is), and believe that He loves you.

My life of song and dance would never be the same. I meditate with grief renewed upon this event that so changed my life and my relationship to God. And yet... This was His promise to me:

"I believe that I should look upon the goodness of the Lord in the land of the living! Wait for the Lord; be strong, and let your heart take courage; wait for the Lord!"
Psalm 27:13-14 (ESV)

He, the great I Am, the maker and lover of our hearts and souls, is true to His Word, and I have seen His goodness.

"O taste and see that the Lord is good! Blessed is the man who takes refuge in Him!"
Psalm 34:8 (ESV)

I have tasted. And His sweetness consumes my soul. In Him I truly live and breathe and have my being.

Prologue:

I met my husband to be when he was 30 years old and I was 26. Having grown up in the Los Angeles area he was a true California surfer boy. It seems to me that his closet describes him best. At this point in his life, it consisted of Hawaiian print shirts, shorts, (And oh, they were short back in the 1980's) Karachi sandals, and a deer-skin jacket that he saved for Sundays. Not that there's anything wrong with that, it's just that it's not Canadian—which is what I am. I grew up on a grain farm in rural Alberta, Canada. My world consisted of combines, fort building, good books, hockey, and appropriate Sunday clothing. Needless to say, we had very little in common, but love does not recognize cultural borders, nor does it give a rip about our clothes closet.

Roy was attending a school at the U.S. Center for World Mission and I had obtained a three-month visa to attend the same school. We married within nine months and began our life together. There was no doubt in either of our minds that God had called us both to 'ministry', even though we weren't sure what that meant. Roy was a new believer without any religious training and it soon became apparent that we needed to start from scratch and go to Bible school. Thus we moved to Three Hills, Alberta, and attended Prairie Bible College, which was only forty miles from my Dad's farm. I desperately longed to be a mother and finally became pregnant after we had been married just over three years.

The Journal

November 1986

Saturday, November 22

I worked at the computer for 10 hours today, trying to get my term paper done. Two weeks 'till the end of the semester and then the baby. We went to a "Circle of Friendship" (oh, brother—where do they get these names?) game night tonight. Before we left, I told Roy that I hadn't noticed the baby move at all today. He said not to worry. I'm sure he's right. I've been concentrating so hard on this paper; I probably wouldn't have noticed it anyway.

Sunday, November 23

Last night when I went to bed I laid really still and concentrated on feeling the baby move...just for reassurance. Still didn't feel anything. Took an afternoon nap and purposely lay very still again. Still no movement. Sam and Carol came for a surprise visit. Steven is four weeks old. It was so wonderful to hold him and think that in a few short weeks I would be holding my own. These little people will be so close in age. I hope they are good friends. I did mention to Carol that the baby seems to have stopped moving. She thinks maybe I should call my doctor tomorrow just to make sure everything is all right. I'm not worried. I've heard that when you get closer to term, the baby may not move as much. I can't believe the time is almost here! I can't believe that this is happening to us! We are having a baby! Oh, thank you Lord for answering our prayers. I've never wanted anything this much, ever in my life before.

Wednesday, November 26

As I write this down it will seem like this nightmare must be happening to someone else, not to me...except that my surroundings, my aching eyes, head, and heart tell me it's all too real.

Yesterday, I called my doctor, feeling a little embarrassed, sure I was overreacting because it's my first baby. I left a message with the receptionist to ask Dr. McPherson to call me. When she called back she asked me to meet her at her office at 5:00pm. Everything was routine until she didn't pick up a heartbeat. I was lying on my back and for some reason kept fainting. She decided to just send me straight over to the hospital and put me on the fetal monitor. I went home, got Roy and ran downstairs to Barry and Maine's apartment to let them know that I thought the baby was under stress. My guess was they might do a C-section. Barry and Maine were having dinner, celebrating their second anniversary, and promised to pray for us.

At the hospital they still didn't pick up a heartbeat and I could tell from Dr. McPherson's face that she was concerned. She got on the phone to the city and talked to a specialist. They decided I should go right to the city where they could do an ultrasound to pick up the heartbeat. We came into the case room in emergency. Everyone did seem pretty grave. Dr. McPherson was with us. They tried their instruments first, but nothing. While we were waiting for the technician to come do the ultrasound, Dr. McPherson said, "I need to warn you that there is a 95% chance your baby is dead." She and the other doctor left the room. We waited in silence. The technician eventually arrived, did the ultrasound and simply said, "There's no fetal movement; I'm sorry, the baby's dead." And without another word, she walked out and left Roy and I completely alone. We looked at each other, stunned. Eventually, we were ushered back to the case room and our weeping or wailing or however you describe the first groanings of despair, started. We tried, incoherently, to make plans. What do you do with a pregnant lady who is carrying around a dead baby? We weren't sure. We needed someone to tell us. It was about 10:40pm.

We called Mum and Dad. They were shattered. Arrangements were made for me to stay in the hospital because, of course, the baby needed to be born. Monday night was the hardest for me. Roy stayed until about midnight and being together was such a comfort. They gave me a sedative so I could sleep but it didn't work. It was just impossible to stop thinking. Finally I called the nurse to find out if it was almost morning so I could get up. It was only

3:00am. She made me some tea and took my blood pressure. She was weeping and the tears dripped off her nose. She will never know how much those tears meant to me. I read my Bible and cried…read my Bible and cried…I called the nurse's station again to find out what time it was—only 5:30am. So I read and cried some more and finally fell asleep only to be woken at 7:30am to have four big tubes of blood taken. To understate it: it was the longest night of my life. Roy came over again at 10:00am. That morning Mum and Dad, the Olvers, Pastor George, and Pastor Herb came. At noon they injected something into my cervix to try and ripen it to induce labour. I had to lie still for three hours. They checked my blood pressure every fifteen minutes—not very conducive to rest. In the afternoon Kathryn came followed by Barry and Maine. I really didn't want a lot of visitors but was glad to see my family. We just sat in silence, which is the only sound I wanted to hear.

That evening they moved me to a room that was not in the maternity ward, for which I was grateful. All night long I had listened to the cries of newborn babies. Their cries and mine, mixed together…all night. What a living hell. I'm now in a nice private room that overlooks an indoor courtyard filled with plants and trees. Today they have been inducing me again but in tablet form—two, every hour, for ten hours. I think I'm starting to feel slight contractions (it's 9:00pm) but it's really hard to know since I've never been in labour before. I'm bleeding. Now what does that mean? I'm praying the baby will come tomorrow. I'm so scared. Kathy came and we visited —no, we cried. She knows there is nothing to say— just cry—and we did.

Thursday, November 27

So many emotions have engulfed me. I hardly know where to begin to write down my feelings. The grief has been more intense that anything I've experienced before, more than simple words can express—it's coming from depths I never knew I had—it seems bottomless yet somehow it's not unbearable. No, that's not it exactly. There's an ebb and a flow, and wax and a wane. Something or Someone is keeping me from breaking that fragile thread of sanity to insanity. That's what I mean when I say that somehow it's not unbearable. The temptation is there…to let go and never come back. To just stop altogether. To lose myself in this bottomless darkness. But, somehow, I keep coming up for air. Its expression—the roll upon swelling roll of grief—isn't there a deeper word?—no, grief is the only word we've been given to describe it. The roll upon roll of grief is the only way I'm kept from stepping over the edge. I don't know how I'm still able to live. How can it be that my heart is still beating when my soul is dead?

"It is of the Lord's mercies we are not consumed."
Lamentations 3:22a (KJV)

Surely His hand is on me or I would die.

I'm so exhausted tonight I can't even go through all the emotion of writing down my emotions. Besides that, I'm struggling for words. I try to write but I can only feel. My weak attempts will have to wait until tomorrow. Tonight I need to just experience. It's 10:00pm and my faithful Roy is still here working on his Greek. We're listening to John Michael Talbot's "To the Great Musician" in the background and it's very comforting. I haven't felt any contractions this hour... it doesn't look like labour will happen tonight. Oh Lord, please tomorrow…

Saturday, November 29

It's Saturday, and we are at Mum and Dads, and for the moment enjoying a quiet house. Dad went to work on the farm early this morning, Mum is having a rest and Roy is doing homework. We are still waiting for the baby to come. I spent all day Thursday hooked up to an IV of cytosine but labour did not come. Now I must wait until Wednesday and they'll hook me up again—unless labour comes naturally before that. I'm in a bit of pain today. It hurts when I move. Last night I had cramps that were much like my period. I suppose this is all part of the labouring process.

This whole experience is so deeply, deeply spiritual. I've had many thoughts that I've never had before. Who could possibly know my mind except God? I feel surrounded by Him, shielded. I sense His presence with me in both mind and heart. In His Word He speaks to me and comforts me—so many promises of His presence. The world doesn't exist. It's just me and God. Only He knows; and I feel like He knows completely.

My pain is so deep; I am unable to express it. I have no words. I keep saying that. I can't quite grasp the fact that there is no language for the bowels of the soul. I never knew that before. God understands my heart and speaks to me. There is nothing, no one but God to be present in my depths, nothing, no one to ease my pain.

Dad told me tonight, with tears in his eyes, he would gladly go through labour for me if he could. I know he would; but he can't. He loves me so much.

Lord, we have *given this child to you* from the day we first knew of its existence. I know this death is not a mistake (even though it seems like it must be). This death is not a mistake because our lives are in your sovereign hands. This baby, our firstborn, has gone back to you…back to that time that is both before and after time. I've thought a lot about Hannah, how she prayed for a child (just like I did) and then she gave him back to you as an act of worship. How? How was that an act of worship? Do I have to do that? I don't think you killed my child in my womb as a sacrifice of worship. Our stories are not the same. Yet, somehow, (if you will only show me) I do want to worship you through or in spite of this death. Please don't ever allow my grief to exceed my worship (I don't even know why I'm talking about worship except that you are here with me and I know it). It's hard to make sense of it all and at this point. Show me.

I'm scared of bitterness. It's already lurking there, ready to sweep in and destroy me (so soon!). I trust you and know that you are not unjust. That is not consistent with what I know to be true about your character. This death does not change who you are. You are still good. Father, I know you understand and are not angry with me when I want to die. You look at me only in graciousness.

It's just that it's hard to think that I've so joyfully carried this child for nine months, loved and nurtured it only to lose it. The baby is so real because I'm still carrying it (is it a boy? a girl?) yet it is dead! It is with you now. Is it with you? He, She…better be! or I will for sure lose all hope to live. And, even in death what is there? Do I want to see my baby more than I want to see you? Right now, yes. The answer is yes. I'm sorry. They are all such strange, devastating, yet fantastic thoughts.

The child was always yours—how glibly we say such things—we knew that from the start and must now prove that we meant it. But why, why did our child come and then leave? What's the point here? I don't get it, but when I see your face Lord, I know I'll understand. Here, there is no understanding. Don't try, anyone, to give me answers. There are NONE. Until then—I trust you. I really do. Help me to never doubt you. I'm so often, in my darkness, tempted. Protect me from the enemy. Protect me from the enemy of my devastated soul from whence, I've discovered, come the utterances that are unutterable.

Do not let me doubt your love and the truth of your character.

Lord, be with Roy. It's so hard for me to see him grieve. I know he wants to be strong for me yet I know he is hurting so badly inside.

<u>December 1986</u>

Tuesday, December 2

Tomorrow morning at 7:15am I go to the hospital and they will try to induce labour—again. Tonight I have been having mild contractions and I have been spotting all day. I just pray the labour comes naturally —I don't look forward to the IV. They can never find a vein.

So many people have called to say they are praying for us—such support and love. I'm grateful. How you will answer their prayers remains to be seen, but you are certainly giving us strength. I guess that's an answer. I feel your presence in my spirit—in my hidden depths where no one exists but you, me, and the baby. I have no doubt that tomorrow will be a hard day but you haven't given me grace for tomorrow yet. I have grace for tonight and that is sufficient. I pray for the grace to go through this labour, and grace to see our baby who will be lifeless. I've never seen a dead body before. Help me.

It's a strange feeling to know it's all over before it has begun. We, and most of those around me, know the baby is dead but it hasn't even been born yet. It's mixed up. The timing is wrong. We're not suppose to mourn before the person has even lived! Sometimes I feel like this is all a dream and I will wake up soon or like this must be happening to someone else—not me. Roy and I have talked a lot about what we would feel like if our child were handicapped in some way. Just because we are Christians does not mean we are exempt from tragedy and heartbreak. Why shouldn't it happen to us as well as to anyone else? Babies die; some are born mentally incompetent; some are deformed. It happens every day. For some reason death was chosen by God for our baby.

Death has become the very thing that makes me human. Human suffering—this is the veil lifted. Welcome to life, Norma. I can see already that grief opens some unknown deep. We are layered. The soul must be an artisan well because I can't see the bottom of my grief. And I feel like my grief is coming from my soul. I've become a different person in just a few short days. I feel like I'm getting to know myself, my real self. Not that anyone else would see it, but I know it. I understand God more; no, not understand, but I sense the infinite. I understand life more, and now hope for the infinite. Not that I could explain it if someone asked. I just know that I am different on the inside. I've turned a corner somewhere and discovered a different world—a secret world. If only I can continually walk through this with you Jesus— take my hand. I'm scared.

I've always said (WORDS, WORDS, WORDS! I'm sick of them! How easily I've talked.) Nevertheless, I've always said that the world needs to see faith (unshakeable confidence in the character of God) more than it needs to see signs and wonders. Now is my hour for faith—yet it too is a gift from you. Please give it to me Jesus. Prove my big words true. I am confident in your love and your faithfulness. You are unchangeable and I trust you, even in this death. Sustain me in my human grief. Why you made us so is a mystery to me at this point. I am bursting—I am numb.

Thank you for the hope of the infinite. Thank you for becoming finite so that I could live with infinite hope. Thank you for being totally selfless—so unlike me. Keep me from feeling secure in the concern and attention of others—that will end—may my only hope be in you.

Saturday, December 6

Well, I suppose it's all over now. I wish my mind and heart would know that. Today is Saturday, Levi Nielsen Bennett was born at 7:35 on Wednesday morning, December 3, 1986. Now I can stop saying *it* and call him *he*. I like that. I started mild contractions at 9:00pm Tuesday night and by midnight they were getting stronger. I decided to try sleep and if it was real labour I was sure the contractions would keep me awake. About 1:30am I told Roy I was getting up to time the contractions again.

We called the hospital and went in around 3:30am. When we arrived at emergency a nurse said, "Oh, how exciting! Is it your first?" I just stared at her. I couldn't think of a thing to say (except to call her an idiot although I guess I knew she'd done nothing wrong). I now started to concentrate on my breathing and the nurse said I was dilated two cm. I knew the baby was actually coming! What an experience.

I asked the Lord to help me not lose control by thinking too much. I needed to concentrate on my breathing. This was not the time for weeping but for working. Roy was incredible! When I went into active labour he was right there to breathe with me. When the desire came to push and I couldn't I don't know what I would have done without him to help me breathe—I couldn't remember how—the pain was so intense. I vomited three times in between breathing into poor Roy's yellow face.

Finally, the doctor said I could push with the contractions. What a relief. What a strange sensation to feel the baby come out (and everything else too!). Levi had lost a lot of weight since he had died 11 days earlier. I also had lost about four lbs. Levi only weighed 4lbs, 10oz at birth. The doctor said he would have been an eight to nine lbs. baby had he not died. Even at 4lbs, 10oz he didn't look skinny.

I appreciated how careful the nurse was with him. She wrapped him in a blanket and gently cradled him in her arm as she brought him to me. He had deteriorated quite a bit in my womb and it was hard to tell whom he looked like. He was ours and I loved him—my baby son.

As far as they could tell the cord had not caused a problem although it may have kinked just long enough to cut off air supply. The postmortem report was rather vague as there were no living cells to do tests on. They are not giving us any answers.

Levi was buried yesterday in the same burial plot with Grandma Nielsen. She would have liked that. Several people think we should have a memorial service but Roy and I are so exhausted emotionally (and physically) that we don't feel capable of such an endeavour. We are telling ourselves, "Maybe in the spring, after the thaw, when we lay his tombstone."

I didn't even stay in the hospital overnight after his birth. I was back home at Mum and Dads' by 7:00pm. I was lying on the couch drifting in and out of sleep while Dad was reading the paper and Roy was studying. Every now and then they would talk and I would catch pieces of their conversation. They both love me so much—how fortunate I've been with my men.

I had a terrible experience the day after Levi's birth. Roy wanted to do something special for me so he took me to the mall to pick out a new dress. I didn't really want to go, partly because I was in pain and partly because I just wanted to hide from the world for a while. Because this is the town I grew up in, I was afraid I would run into someone I knew and I didn't want to talk.

Well, it happened. While paying for the dress, a woman who I knew looked at me and said, "So when is your baby due?" (I realize I didn't look so wonderful but did I really still look pregnant?) I couldn't believe her stupid question. I turned away from her, put my money on the counter and said, "He was born yesterday and he's dead." As I walked out I glanced at her and she was looking at her friend, laughing! How could she?! She's laughing at me for still looking pregnant and because she made the mistake of asking. 'Miss glamour girl' can't imagine anything worse than to still look pregnant when you're not. What about the baby!? Didn't you hear me say the baby was DEAD! She walked off still whispering to her friends. I hate her. How can she be so incredibly superficial?! I want her to hurt 'till she wishes for death.

Then we met Carol on an outing with Steven in the stroller. Carol, of course, was very surprised to see me and her eyes immediately filled with tears as we talked. I couldn't bring myself to even once glance at the baby. While we were talking Sue came up to us. She talked about everything except my baby (even though she knew very well). When she left, Carol said, "Was she on drugs?" No, she's just an idiot.

It was a nice thought, but it was a stupid idea to go to the mall. (I didn't let Roy know I felt that way. He only wanted to ease my pain.)

The few days that have passed since Levi's birth have been difficult. Roy went home yesterday to pack up the baby things and take down the crib. Everything had been ready since I was just three months pregnant. I couldn't bear going home and putting it all away. Not that it was easy for Roy. I came home today.

So here we are. I am a mother with no baby. Life seems very grey and commonplace right now. We were both sitting in the study earlier hard at work—I just had to go lie on my bed after a while and cry and cry at the sameness of everything. We have gone through two weeks of letting go of the most precious thing God had given us. Now we're back to studies—almost as if nothing has happened. Life can be so full of love, hopes, and dreams one minute and then all of a sudden it's completely empty. We're back to the factory, the assembly line, just punching out duties. I don't even know what I'm doing; I'm just doing it. I may as well be a robot.

Time goes on but how can I? Our first-born son: Levi. I love to say his name. We are parents. But we are hollow, empty, vacant, and void.

I'm glad to have had the experience of giving birth. That work was just me and Levi; me and Levi, just we two.

Sunday, December 7

Today was Sunday but I stayed home from church. I can't bear the church people. With very few exceptions, we have been ignored and avoided. Why are they so afraid of me? We can talk about everything except heartache. My world just ended and the whole church is silent. No, that's not true. David and Rosalie have not been silent. They have expressed sorrow, and also admitted that they feel helpless. Those are good, true words. If one more person says, "God never gives us more than we can handle," I'll probably hit them. Salt in the wound, using scripture to rub it in. This pastoral internship, however, is a nightmare.

We spent the day writing a newsletter and thank you notes. We should have been sending out baby announcements. We have received so many flowers and cards it's just been unbelievable. I'm going to make a scrapbook in memory of Levi (my baby book).

Thank God that the future holds the promise of seeing him and knowing him. Death is not final. But oh how human you have made us. How attached to humanity we are and how deeply love flows.

Right now I'm wondering if there is a future for me. I see no future. Seems like all I can do is cry. It's only been four days and the memory is still so fresh (I don't want to lose this memory; I want to cling to it, live with it, die with it). I am realizing that there is nothing that will fill the empty void of not having my little son. Being pregnant again won't make everything better. Lord, I need you to come and fill this fathomless pit. Be bigger than my heart. Be bigger than this pit. I said Levi was yours. My life is hidden in you. I want no part exposed to the world or I will die. Your Word is my solace alone and I cling to it.

> *"He will cover you with his feathers, and under his wings you will find refuge; his faithfulness will be your shield and rampart.*
> *You will not fear the terror of night..."*
> Psalm 91:4-5a (NIV)

I'm fearful. Cover me.

Friday, December 12
Today we finished our exams and this semester is over. However did I do it? It was dreadful going back to school. Of course the whole college knew what had happened and I felt like a freak on stage. Most people didn't say anything and just ignored me.

All I want to do is cry yet my grief is so private I don't want to share it with anyone. Who could understand? I go through the days with colossal headaches from holding back the tears. And then someone (a friend) addresses my grief and I fall apart. I think I'd like a year just to be by myself and cry.

And yet, there are times when I want to talk about the experience, not just the grief. I want to talk about the delivery. It was difficult and yet we accomplished it. Such grace you give Lord. Thank you for Maine and Kathy. They have sat by the hour and listened to me talk. They've cried and they've let me cry. How I love them.

Saturday, December 13
Wrote this in my notebook while in English class:
I am a mother now,
But mothering is not to be my privilege.
I am a mother now,
But God chose to take home that which was already His.

(I promised him he could when I told him, "This is your child" I didn't know what I was saying.)
My son was not meant to make his home here on

earth.
> God created him,
>> Watched him grow in my womb,
>>> Listened to our prayers for him,
>>>> Saw how we loved him...

Then...
Gave him life only to be lived in heaven.
How important his little life must be...
Our little Levi.
That you want him now. (That doesn't make sense, I'm just looking for reason...is there any?)
 You gave him to me for nine months—
>> To be snuggled tight in my womb and receive all the love a mother could possible give. (I didn't know this kind of love existed.)

And then...he was gone.
> (I didn't know this kind of grief existed.)

His presence in heaven was not a surprise to you,
Your eye has been on us since his conception.
I am a mother now.
I share a secret with God. I speak to him; he speaks to me.
I am a mother now.
But I've given my son to Jesus...
>> No, I didn't give him; you took him; and now you are asking me to give him.
>>> (Sigh. It wouldn't have been my choice, Jesus, but that is what you've asked of me.)

YOU are holding him now. Please...hold me, too.

Tuesday, December 16

We are in Banff tonight. We decided to take a few days and get away by ourselves. Friends offered us a room at their motel, which has been wonderful, as we never could have afforded this retreat.

Tonight we went out for supper and splurged—steak and lobster—our fourth anniversary dinner. It was nice to sit and talk. Afterwards we went swimming back at the motel with Cam and Kathryn. She told me that she's four months pregnant. I'm the first person she's told. She found it hard—she didn't want to hurt me. I cried and she cried. It's been hard for her to watch me lose our baby when she's been pregnant all this time. More babies in the family. It doesn't help that my large family is such a baby factory.

<u>January 1987</u>

Thursday, January 1

I have so many thoughts I want to write down but it seems I always get interrupted. Maybe tonight I can stop and think through things again.

It has been almost five weeks since Levi was born. I still think about him every moment. People think I'm living—I am not. I'm a hollow shell who has attached mechanical parts to my person. I'm Frankenstein inside out.

It seems there have been babies everywhere we go lately. I find those are my hardest times and I still can't bring myself to look at a baby. It makes me feel so empty. It's such an ache. I want to hold and love my own little baby so badly. Once again, it's too deep to express.

> *"I am poured out like water, and all my bones*
> *are out of joint. My heart has turn to wax;*
> *it has melted within me."*
> Psalm 22:14 (NIV)

Sometimes it hardly seems possible that all this has happened to me. Every now and then I'll run into someone who thinks lightly of our loss and will say, "Oh well, you'll have another," or "you're still young," or "it's not the end of the world." They have no idea. I can hardly bear to be civil with them. Are they even human? I don't think so.

Yet, when I look back I am stunned at the grace you gave us to go through it all. I still need your grace to face the new mothers, new babies and excited mothers-to-be. When I hear someone is pregnant, I think, "Wait. Don't get excited. There are no guarantees." I went to the doctor today and she said my body is ready to get pregnant again. (Even though I think I still look awful.) I can't even think about it.

Christmas break is over and school starts again tomorrow. I'm looking forward to it. I've got to do something. I'm only taking four classes and hope to have more time to spend with my girlfriends. They are a gift from you, God. Thanks.

Christmas didn't really even happen this year (at least for me). I had such wonderful daydreams about having a baby for Christmas. Instead it was a nightmare.

Be true to your promise:

"The Lord is close to the brokenhearted and saves those who are crushed in spirit."
Psalm 34:18 (NIV)

This is me, Lord. Be close. Save me.

Monday, January 12
Roy is at a seminar tonight for his Bachelor of Theology paper. I was reading through my

hermeneutics notes but fell asleep so I thought I'd retire to my bed and write a bit.

It's been almost six weeks since Levi's birth. Laura's little boy said this about his fathers death: "It hurts so bad I just want to explode inside!" Agreed. I've actually made it through a couple of days without visible tears. I can't stop thinking of him though. I'm continually weeping inside. It's like everything right now is filtered through Levi first. All of life, all... It's hard to explain.

I hate being on this campus! I can't get away from all the reminders. Babies and expectant mothers bring so much attention and in my heart I am jealous and resentful.

I'm not getting this, Lord. I don't understand why you took Levi. You knew how much I wanted him. Or maybe 'wants' don't matter to you. There aren't any answers, are there? There's just you. I've never felt such intense, sickening... grief—that is the word, isn't it? It's not enough. One word is not enough. There is no word...

I suppose there's much I can learn from this and you have your purposes and you're loving, and all those other nice things I could say about you. But honestly, Lord, that is not very consoling right now. I'm having trouble with you.

Today, I typed a letter for Roy that he wrote to Woody. In it he said, "It hurts so good." What a load of crock! He can't possibly mean that and I suspect he only wrote it because that's what Woody would want him to say. Roy is not hurting good; he is hurting bad.

How do you spiritualize pain? "Causing all things to work together for good" doesn't make a lick of sense to me right now. My heart's been ripped open. If I talk about it, people think I'm dwelling on the past and must go on. (At least that's what I feel they must be thinking; it's what I would have thought. Oh that everyone could walk a mile in grief's shoes. How silent we would be.)

Levi is like my own cherished memory now. He seems forgotten by the world around. I don't care. They never understood anyway. He is mine…oh…I just thought of Tolkien's "My Precious." I'm not ready to explore that thought yet, but maybe in the future.

The thought of another pregnancy is no comfort at all. Pregnancy is just an illusion—babies don't really come from pregnancy. Nine months seemed so long with Levi and I don't want to go through that again and still have no baby.

I know you say that you only give us what we have the grace to handle (is your grace really unlimited? It must be since I am still sane) but please, God, don't do it again. I know you want me to be strong and I want to be strong but, oh God, it's so hard to think about losing another baby. Give me grace—that's all I'm asking for. I can't handle my thoughts. They go wild with tragic imaginings. What else might happen? Anything! Everything! We are not exempt. Once again, I feel on the edge. Insanity sleeps in bed with me. I could go there in a heartbeat, Lord. Don't let me. If I let go...

I hope you're enjoying Levi—I don't mean that sarcastically. There must have been a purpose for his existence (mustn't there?). I ache for him because I'm so, so, human. He was in my heart (and will stay there for my lifetime) and in my womb for nine months. What wonderful and joyful months they were. Carrying Levi in my womb was the most beautiful thing that has ever happened to me. I even enjoyed the discomfort of being big. It didn't matter, I was pregnant. I cherish the memory. My little boy brought me so much happiness, but now the happiness is equalled in grief. They are really so much the same: happiness and grief. How can that be? I loved him so much. Oh Lord, I feel so empty— fill me with something. I need more than I am. My soul is wandering like a phantom looking for a home. Your presence, your grace, YOU! I am empty again.

> "*My soul melts away for sorrow;*
> *strengthen me according to you word!*"
> Psalm 119:28

I wish now that I had held him in my arms after he was born. I was afraid to. He looked so fragile and I was afraid his little body would fall apart because he had been dead for 11 days. We speculate so much about heaven. I hope I can hold him as a newborn babe in heaven. I want to bond through the eyes not just the heart.

Wednesday, January 21

I've finally had the nerve to do some reading on grief (it's taken two months). Most of the stuff out there gives answers that are too easy. It makes me angry to read it. They try to pacify me with empty words that have no hope. Step 1, 2, 3... They try to give me a formula to "get over my grief." But they don't let me grieve. Shut up. Just shut up. Don't tell me how to do this. Don't give me your insipid answers... they are shallow. I keep going back to the Psalmist. God, you alone have the words of life. C.S. Lewis, <u>A Grief Observed</u> has been good; I don't feel so alone. Like Lewis, I do sometimes feel like I'm going in circles with my grief and I keep rounding the same corner over and over again without going on down the road. My journal is repetitive. I'm standing still, or sometimes whirling, spinning on some kind of grief maypole.

Like the other night at the student wives prayer meeting: Mary Sue was there rejoicing over her wonderful natural childbirth and their darling little daughter, gush, gush... their eighth, or some ridiculous number... until I could have thrown my chair at her. I wanted to vaporize so no one would see me, as the tears just wouldn't stop flowing. Why did I even go? Feeling like a total idiot and hating Mary Sue with all my heart, I finally left the room, came home and cried like I did the first day. I am rounding the same corner over and over.

Am I unspiritual (do I care)? Yes, for hating (and no, I don't care). It's not her I hate exactly. Oh, I'm so frustrated! I can't explain my feelings! Why? Why? Why? I thought I'd dealt with this and understood there was no answer to Why?! It feels like this grief will never end and that my insides will be pickled, cold, and numb for the rest of my life.

Roy has so understood. He never tells me not to cry or that I should be over it by now. It's just the opposite. He wants to be there when I cry and just lets me cry and talk all I want. He's always got time for me to express my grief. What would I do without him? He doesn't try to give me any easy answers either. He doesn't have any.

Then there are days when the revolving door of grief will grant me a slight respite, and I feel like I'm moving forward. But those days are so few and are not days, exactly, but mere moments. Like having a good laugh with Kathy and then I'll realize how long it's been since I laughed.

February 1987

Wednesday, February 25

It's been three weeks since I've written. I was talking to Gloria today and she told me that she is praying for me now more than ever. I really appreciated that. As time goes on, people forget (it's not their grief) and some people I meet now don't even know I was pregnant. The memory is still precious and only God knows my silent pain (pain is not a strong enough word, but I know by now, no word is). People should never say, "I know exactly how you feel." Idiots; of course they don't. Only God can possibly know the depth of the hearts joys and sorrows. I didn't know this before (speaking of idiots) even though I'd read it in the Psalms.

March 1987

Thursday, March 26

Tonight was the "Senior Wives Tea." I'm getting sick of all this stuff. One emotional throw-up after another as they take their turn to say goodbye after four years of school. I kept thinking, "Next year it will be my turn." I tried to imagine what our lives would be like next year. But as I've learned from the last four months—life is not predictable. Is there any other tragedy in store for us? Will we have another child? Will we even graduate? We set our goals and plan our lives as if it was all up to us, forgetting that we are not writing our own biographies. Trouble is, God, can I embrace your story for me?

I've been clinging (clinging, yes, because I'm desperate to attach my grief to words and I certainly have no words to express hope) clinging to this verse, again:

> "*I would have despaired unless I had believed that I would see the goodness of the Lord in the land of the living. Wait for the Lord; be strong and let your heart take courage; yes wait for the Lord.*"
> Psalm 27:13-14 (NASB)

Sometimes I'm despairing, Lord (it's not 'would have

despaired' as the Psalmist said it's 'despairing'—active verb)—especially at times like tonight when mothers give 'testimony of your faithfulness to them' in giving healthy children. I've had thoughts today that I'll need to deal with—selfpity.

Joan and Doug's baby was born with a hole in his heart and probably won't live. My first thought was, "Yeah right. They'll fix the heart and everything will be fine. Everybody's story has a happy ending except mine. Why couldn't someone else lose their baby? Why is life so rosy for everyone else?"

What horrible, selfish thoughts. Yet they are too real to ignore. Oh God, keep me from bitterness. When I heard their baby was dying, I wept for Joan and Doug (or was it for myself? I don't know anymore) and yet I felt they couldn't possibly feel the same grief that I have felt over Levi. They still have four children! (If Levi had been child number four or five would it have made my grief any less? Of course not.) I know I can't judge their grief. It is so individual. I, of all people, should know that.

As the Proverbs says...

"Each heart knows its own bitterness..."
Proverbs 14:10a (NIV)

Help me to learn this lesson (is all this about learning lessons? I don't think so, nevertheless...) help me so that selfpity doesn't ruin my life. It scares me. Their baby hasn't died yet and you may choose to heal and I will have to rejoice with them and not compare their story with mine.

It's like Aslan said to Aravis in The Chronicles of Narnia, "No one is told any story but their own." I'm glad for that. I wouldn't want anyone else to have my story—not because I wouldn't want anyone else to grieve, I just don't want them to have my grief. My grief is precious. There it is again. Precious. Can something precious become the thing that ruins you? Still not ready to think about it too much, but I think, someday, I'll need to.

April 1987

Thursday, April 2

Joan and Doug's baby is fine. Of course. Had a membrane covering a valve to the heart but an operation was all that was needed. So they have their fifth child. I'm happy for them. I guess.

Our blood tests still won't be back for another month. Suppose there is something wrong with either Roy or me? I'll deal with that when I have to.

I was asked to speak at the Alumni rally during conference. (Why is it when someone has *tragedy* in their life they are immediately given their fifteen minutes of fame?) "Supporting One Another" is the topic. I think I can do that. In fact, I think I have something to say about that. I have had so much support from *the girls*. Our Tuesday breakfasts have been the highlight of my week. (Unlike church which I loath.) They have been a big part of my healing process. The girls are so okay with my feeling swings. They let me cry, laugh, talk, whatever I need; they are there without judgement. Everything is so structured in our lives right now with school and I've enjoyed having Tuesday mornings without an agenda. Yet as I look back on our Tuesdays, I see that you had an agenda all along. You have salved my pain through these girlfriends. I must not forget this. I think this is probably more significant than I even understand right now. I think it's part of your grace upon grace... do they know? I don't think so.

Friday, April 17

The other day in the store I ran into Lois. She asked me how I was, but it wasn't the flippant, "Hi, how ya doin'?" It was really "How are you?" She wanted to really know. She said she still prays for me and I know it is true. Her sincerity was written on her face and heard through her voice—and for once, it wasn't the fake head-tilt like so many of them are.

How is it that she still remembers? She seems to know that I'm still raw. Maybe she's a woman who has also suffered. Maybe grief is more common than I realized. Maybe she has that illusive appendage, grief, just hovering over her heart too—a constant, quiet, singular prick... that "thing" that's just between her and God. Maybe there are many people like me. Maybe we all walk around masking the deep. Always keeping the billows at bay.

I don't expect people to remember my little story. We all have our own loves and daily trials. And yet I keep running into people who still remember, who are still praying. Where would I be on this continuum they call "the grieving process" if these people had not prayed? Would I have been able to cope with the last four months on the strength of my own relationship with God? Surely prayer has done more for Roy and me than we will ever know. Really, though, I don't get it. Prayer is such a mystery to me. Would God have given me grace if I was alone and no one knew of my grief? Does God give grace for private pain? Does pain have to be public and *much prayed for* before God steps in and gives you some help? Are prayer requests just for the narcissist? I don't know. I really don't. I asked Roy and his answer was, "we pray because God tells us to." For now, and I think for the rest of my life, this answer will suffice. God says "pray." End of story. God knows my whole existence is just one big prayer right now. That secret world that He and I share is the real world. I live my life in a tunnel of communication with God. The world happens around me, but I'm unaware.

I feel like I have gone through a human experience that we should be too fragile for. How would an unbeliever... I should say, WHO would an unbeliever turn to? I am so empty. I have NOTHING to give myself. There is nothing in me to hold on to.

"My tears have been my food day and night."
Psalm 42:3a (NIV)

Sometimes I've been physically sick with grief and, yes, the pain has been too intense for words. Yet, here I am—loving you Jesus, with all my heart. In fact, knowing you Jesus. Knowing that...

"You hem me in, behind and before...if I go
to the heavens you are there; if I make my
bed in the depths, you are there."
Psalm 139:5a & 139:8 (NIV)

I am finding you everywhere. Far too mysterious a thing to find words for. And, I'm still loving Roy (I've heard that many marriages don't make it through the loss of a child). There are moments when I even have hopes and dreams for the future, and sometimes I'm even excited about life, today. I can't believe I just wrote that! Perhaps grief is a process after all. I don't see the process as a straight line, however. Or maybe it's a straight line but it has no ending. Did it have a beginning? I don't know. It seems that what grief did was open up a part of me that had to have been there all along but it was veiled. Grief has been a layered experience. A layer of me, a layer of God. A deeper layer of me, a deeper layer of God—until its gone so deep I have to stop trying to express it. It's like a deep calling to deep.

I thought in the beginning that grief was a "sort of" spiritual experience. Now I know it is, in its totality, a spiritual experience. That "thing" that "spark" that gives "life" is infinite, and grief can only be experienced within this realm. We were not made for this world, and grief validates both our humanity and our eternalness…joy and sorrow, despair and hope.

This would-be deadly sword has pierced my heart. I am scarred but not dead. No, scarred isn't the right word. I'm more than scarred. It's like I've got a different heart; a different soul—some kind of newness. No, not different, but my soul has been released. It's found home in despair. That's pretty strange.

"My soul thirsts for God..."
Psalm 42:2a (NIV)

It didn't used to. I am a different person. It's like Levi's death brought my rebirth. I will never be the same. I have seen life from the other side. No, it's not a side, it's a depth. I didn't just go from one side to another, I went to the deep and saw a dimension that was "not of this world". I hope I will never be the same. I hope I will always remember the wordless groanings of deep calling to deep.

But back to prayer. Again. Prayer seems like it's such an unseen, non-tactile support yet its answers seem to be evident in the daily grace God provides to live. Maybe prayer isn't a nebulous undefined ritual. It must be the invisible fortress that surrounds the believer. I don't understand it. I know I keep saying that. I just know that, somehow, I am still whole—maybe even more whole because I've become more human. No, not more human, but I've glimpsed my soul somehow. Amazing. Hard to express, of course, and I know I'm writing in circles. Just trying to figure it all out. My own prayers are not so much FOR me...they are more or less wordless...just deep meeting deep. But how much do other people's prayers for me mean? Their prayers at least show that they are trying to enter into my sorrow. Are they suppose to? Did I? Maybe they are putting the words together that I am unable to and they are praying intelligently to God about me. Does God need intelligence? I don't think so. I'm pretty sure He can figure out my groaning.

Saturday, April 25
I've been out of school for a week now. My Greek class continues and I have one spring session. It feels so good to have the pressure off and enjoy being home, riding my bike, and visiting.

I've been chosen for a sort of valedictorian job. I have a year to prepare and present a biography on some significant Christian person. I agreed to it if I could do a drama. I've picked George Muller of Bristol. I love that "Dickens" period of history. I need to have the script written by the fall. I have a lot of work and research ahead of me and I can't wait to get into it. I just wrote "I can't wait."

We are still waiting to get our blood tests back before we can think of getting pregnant again. All these things are in your hands, Lord. I am no longer interested in my own finite mind and its many rabbit-trails. You have so shown yourself to me that I have "unshakable confidence" in your plan—in you. Would I have had this confidence a year ago? I thought I did. I've had my chance to prove it.

I dreamt about babies last night. I imagined holding my own baby close and how he felt. Oh dear. Too overwhelming. I do pray that you would give us another baby. I can't help it. It's my heart's desire.

<u>July 1987</u>

Wednesday, July 29

The summer days are passing quickly and I am busy writing and getting my Production Drama class together.

Today is Levi's nine-month birthday. Pregnancy seemed to move so slowly because I was so excited to see him. This past nine months has seemed to move much faster. Even though I am loath to let my grief fade (fade isn't the right word), I do want to press on and look forward to the future. Sometimes I panic because I'm changing. But that is your grace to me, right? I think it would be sin not to accept your grace, right? The strength I feel in the depths of my soul is not "the grief process changing" it is YOU living with me, living in me, being me... once again, I can't express the oneness I have with you.

> *"I will be glad and rejoice in your love, for you saw my affliction and knew the anguish of my soul. You have not given me into the hands of the enemy but have set my feet in a spacious place."*
> Psalm 31:7-8 (NIV)

The psalmist always finds words when I cannot.
Jesus, it comforts me knowing that you see my

affliction and know the anguish of my soul. I don't bear my grief alone, you understand—we are partners in this grief, sort of betrothed and married in grief. You are the only reason I have not been handed over to the enemy. You have sustained me, understood me and kept me living. You have allowed me to grow so close to you. I know I have never been alone. Your love gives me hope and sets my feet in a spacious place. I thank you, Jesus for your love. I value it above all else and desire nothing else upon earth.

Maine is pregnant! They only tried for one month. Jesus, I'm starting to spin. Hold me. Help me deal and respond rightly at every moment with Barry and Maine. Maine and I had a good talk on Friday. I need to be true to her and never make her feel like I think you are being unfair to me. Help me not to fear the future before it is here. I have trouble thinking about what it will be like when she brings the baby home.

Oh God, if it is what you have for us, I pray I could at least be pregnant. I wish I could quit asking. All my big talk—do I really trust you? Yes, how could I not. I know you.

Today in the Psalms you answered my cry:

"Therefore let all the faithful pray to you while you may be found...

(God, I'm praying to you for YOU, not for SOMETHING!)

...surely the rising of the mighty waters will not

*reach them. You are my hiding place; you will protect
me from trouble and surround me with songs of
deliverance. I will instruct you and teach you in the
way you should go; I will counsel you with my loving
eye on you... The Lord's unfailing love surrounds the
one who trusts in Him."*
Psalm 32:6-10 (NIV)

How could I live without your Words?

Oh, Lord! Writing this verse down... I just thought of something! I've got to go to the field and walk and then I'll try to write down what I'm thinking. I'm blown away...

Okay. So all this time I've been struggling to find words. I haven't found them because I DON'T HAVE THEM! YOU ALONE HAVE THE WORDS OF LIFE! Words! Oh God! I get it! I've not been able to find the words because I don't have them. YOU DO! I can't believe this just happened.

I would have never been able to express my grief except through you. Your words are not only balm to my weak and quivering soul they are the very thing—the heart-beat, the blood infusion, the essence, of my being. Your words are the expression of all that I was, am, and ever will be. I am IN you. I am hidden in Christ, bought with a price, kept by his hand. The mighty waters did not reach me, even in grief, because you kept pulling me higher. I didn't drown because your words gave voice to my soul. I cried to you...I had to cry because I didn't have words; and you answered me... with words. YOUR WORDS

I've got to think about this. I'm going to the field again.

<u>Ode to the Field</u>
My Field—
Your simplicity provides a respite for my cluttered soul.
My eyes are deficient —
          I need the eyes of heaven
          Just to grasp the beauty of the earth.

My feet pull me deeper and
          My cares
                    Are left
                              Strewn
                                        In the field
                                   Behind
I am drawn by the invisible strength that has belonged to this land since the dawn of time.

It is old; I am young
It is strong; I am frail
It is settled; I am restless

I stand still and let the wind tear at the gauze that shrouds my being.

My Field—
I cannot comprehend your essence. It is too much for me.
You are harmonious; I am discordant

I am hungry
 Eat.
I am thirsty
 Drink.
My Field. Gift of God.
 Thank you, God, for sometimes revealing yourself in something other than words. I'm worn out by my own words.

<u>August 1987</u>

Thursday, August 6

The last two days have been rather difficult. Gus Van Geissen died August 3 (exactly nine months after Levi was born). We found out he had cancer the same week we found out Levi had died. Ann has gone through a very difficult nine months as she watched her beloved die a slow and painful death. We were over there the night before the funeral. The whole family was there. We had a good visit and Ann talked (it's so important to be able to do that. I'll forever be grateful to Maine and Kathy for sitting and listening to me for hours. I needed so badly to talk about Levi and his death). Talking with Ann brought back so many memories of Levi. I just cried and cried. Oh how precious heaven is to those whose hearts are already there.

Gus's funeral was yesterday and we went to it all—service, graveside, and luncheon. Last night Roy and I went for a walk in the field and he expressed my same thoughts. Even though this funeral was for Gus, for us it was for Levi. Very strange. For some reason this funeral seemed to be a very precious time to say goodbye and recognize where he was. All day yesterday I had the words to the song, <u>Does Jesus</u>

<u>Care?</u> running through my head. Then they sang it at the funeral. I wept and wept. The professor behind me knew. He touched my shoulder with his hand, but his gesture touched my heart.

<u>Does Jesus Care?</u>
Frank E. Graeff

Does Jesus care when my heart is pained
Too deeply for mirth or song,
As the burdens press, and the cares distress,
And the way grows weary and long?

Refrain:
Oh, yes, He cares, I know He cares!
His heart is touched with my grief;
When the days are weary, the long nights dreary,
I know my Saviour cares.

Does Jesus care when my way is dark
With a nameless dread and fear?
As the daylight fades into deep night shades,
Does He care enough to be near?

Does Jesus care when I've tried and failed
To resist some temptation strong;
When for my deep grief, there is no relief,
Though my tears flow all the night long?

Does Jesus care when I've said "goodbye"
To the dearest on earth to me,

And my sad heart aches till it nearly breaks—
Is it aught to Him? Does He see?

Yes, Lord, I know you care. I am so grateful.
*"Your eye is on the sparrow and I
know He watches me"*.

Tuesday, August 11
I've been meditating on Romans 8:35, 37-39:

*"Who shall separate us from the love of Christ?
Shall trouble or hardship or persecution or famine
or nakedness or danger or sword? ...No, in all
these things we are more than conquerors through
Him who loved us. For I am convinced that
neither death nor life, neither angels nor demons,
neither the present nor the future, nor any powers,
neither height nor depth, nor anything else in
all creation, will be able to separate us from the
love of God that is in Christ Jesus our Lord."*

I don't just read this verse anymore. I know it. These
are the Words of Life.

Saturday, August 15
We had tea with Barry and Maine last night. I could
tell something was on Barry's mind—he was so
meditative. He said that they are realizing what it cost
us to lose Levi. Since Maine has been pregnant they
understand it more. I know what he means—I
thought that would happen—the *reality* of a live baby

in Maine's womb is different than the *idea* of Levi in mine. He expressed how they want to be sensitive to us and not just talk babies all the time. But, didn't Maine listen to me talk, and talk? She'll need to have times to talk and I'd better be just as wonderful to her as she was to me. However, I appreciate Barry's thoughts so much. How fortunate we are to have such family. We love them too much to be jealous. We will try to love and be committed through both the good and the bad times. Neither of our stories is finished.

Sunday, August 16

I wrote a poem that I am going to use as a song for Mary Mueller to sing in the drama. She and her husband are talking about how God is moulding them and giving them compassion through the death of their two-year-old son. I think her feelings must have been similar to mine:

In private pain I've quietly wept;
I've wondered that love could reach such depth.
The sickle of grief left my heart in ruins…
Then He opened His hands and I saw His wounds.

My eyes've been dull, my smile just for show;
I've wondered humanity such pain should know.
I've been chased by selfpity and questions and fears…
Then I looked in His eyes and saw His tears.

Oh God, I still love you though suffering be mine;

My heart in yours hidden and my hand in Thine.
My dreams are your secrets, my hopes understood...
Please take my grief and work it for good.

Thursday, August 20

This past week has been a hard one (I seem to keep saying that). I had convinced myself I was pregnant because my period was seven days late. I have never had that happen before except when I WAS pregnant! How discouraging. I keep telling myself not to live from month to month but with my periods so messed up it's hard not to notice them. I admit Lord, I find it hard that I'm not pregnant. Margie called this morning—she's pregnant—what else??

What do you have for us Lord? Are we not to have children? I need to fight this vicious enemy of selfpity again today. Help me to focus on you—what do I know about you? You are just and true. Eternity is in your eyes and a finite length of years is all I can see. I am so earth bound. Sometimes I forget what I have waiting for me when, at last, my eyes will be opened to your reality—the only reality. You will be seen face to face. My eyes will look upon you, they will no longer be veiled by this earth's atmosphere of doubt and faithlessness. Oh how I long to see you Jesus, and love you with greater understanding. I want to so trust you that I am not swayed by the circumstances around me. Deepen my heart, my being. I want to be embedded in Who You Are! I want to have a voice that declares Your Faithfulness to those around me. Will I ever have words to say what I've discovered about you? Do I even want to?How I treasure the oneness I have found with you. I want to love in the hope of your presence and experience your peace while we fellowship in my soul. Let me be happy in you alone. May I be able to rejoice with others because I have a happy, contented, God-focused heart. Oh God, my heart is so far from bitterness toward you—I love you and trust what you're doing in Roy's and my life. Make me strong. Make me real. Keep me dependent on you. Surely this is your grace to me. Flood me with grace upon grace, roll after roll, for the rest of my life. Because I know you now, I can't bear a moment not in your presence.

<u>September 1987</u>

Saturday, September 5

I have had so many emotions this last week. (Oh, how unusual!) Rachel called and told me Liz is pregnant. She was all excited and of course thought I should be too. The more she talked the harder it was not to cry. Finally, I was crying so hard I couldn't respond to her anymore so I told her I needed to go. She just said, "I'm sorry I upset you." I don't think Rachel understands (understatement). She has always equated my stillbirth with her three-month miscarriage. I know I can't possibly critique her loss, but, give me a break, Rachel! I think the two events were different. The grief may have been similar; although right now I don't think anyone on earth has ever grieved as deeply as I. (I wonder if that's a common feeling.) She thinks she has known all along *exactly* how I'm feeling but it's obvious to me that she doesn't.

Blah...blah... pregnant women talking babies all around me. If I hear one more platitude like, "God knows" I will throw up! I know God knows for heavens sake! And while that gives me more comfort and peace than *they* will ever know—I still hurt and I still grieve that we don't have our baby boy bringing life to our sometimes boring home.

So often when I'm busy or just reading, I think how wonderful it would be to have Levi to care for. This is a difficult stage for me. I am thirty years old and everyone my age is having families. It's talked about all the time and I am excluded from the conversation. I don't count because we have no children (I hate saying that) and I'm not pregnant. Right now four of my closest friends are pregnant. I am surrounded with happy excited mothers and why shouldn't they be? I was too! (Was I an idiot? Was there someone in my world while I was pregnant who was grieving the loss of a child or who was dealing with infertility? I probably wouldn't have noticed. Well, that will change.) It's not that I resent their happiness, it just reminds me how much death hurts and that I am still hurting.

I was talking to Liz today about how hard it is for me when people ask us if we have children (because the school year is just starting, there are lots of new students who don't know me). I have begun to say "no" because if I tell them about my stillbirth they somehow feel obligated to find an answer for it. Some of their "answers" are just ignorant and cruel. By saying, "no", however, I'm saying Levi doesn't exist and that breaks my heart. Liz suggested I say, "Yes, we have a son with the Lord and I would prefer not to talk about it." That's a little too dramatic. It leaves people with imaginations running wild and they would probably ask some one else what happened and then be on eggshells around me. If only there was some way I could just say, "yes, but he's with the Lord," and leave it at that—cut the conversation off somehow without being rude. Somehow I don't think talking about Levi will ever be easy.

I really hope I can get through this month without thinking about my period. I made the mistake of telling Jill when my period was due last month and everyday she was phoning to ask me if it had come. That was stupid—I won't do that again.

Tuesday, September 8

Maine is in the hospital. She is cramping and bleeding. They are not saying yet that she is miscarrying but I know she is. It's hard. Kelly just had her baby and is in the hospital too, which makes it even harder. When I took Maine's things in to her tonight, I hugged her and we cried. She said, "I know I have no right to cry after all you've gone through." I assured her she had every right and of course she should cry–and I mean it. And Barry... he's hurting, too. This is hard for everyone. I guess tonight will tell us exactly what is going on. Sometimes life makes me weary.

Monday, September 21

It's been a long time since I've written. Now that school has started I've become busy again. Maine did lose her baby, I rushed her into the city (Barry was at the farm) and helped her breath as she went through three hours of contractions. What a heartbreaking experience.

I've been thinking a lot the last two weeks about children and just what God may have for us. Maybe it would be best for me to think that we are not going to have any more children. I've never really felt old before but I do now—almost 31—guess it's not old. Maybe I won't get pregnant again. I need to see that my life could still hold interest for me even without children. I guess the most difficult thing is to live with women my age who are mothers. I'm starting to see that I need to focus my life around something other than motherhood. Maybe God's story for me is different.

I'm excited about what I've got ahead of me this year with my drama class. I want to have my heart into what the future holds for me, and not watching every month for my period to come (it just came two days ago—early this month—can't win).

October 1987

Saturday, October 10

Today we are going to the city for Thanksgiving dinner with the family. Steven just had his first birthday and it brought back so many sad reminders of what I was missing. A year will soon be here since Levi was born. Ten months ago, I never dreamed I wouldn't be pregnant now. There are times when I wish we would pursue adoption. I would almost rather not go through another pregnancy. Give us wisdom as to what to do, Lord. It would cost about $3000 to adopt. Yikes! I guess even that is unthinkable for us.

Wednesday, October 21

There is a beautiful pre-winter sunrise this morning. Makes me meditate on the presence of God and the presence of Levi with Him. Beauty and sorrow: both are breathtaking and the essence of each stays with us forever. Levi's headstone was delivered here this morning (a man at the school made it for us). I had a sense, while watching the sunrise, of just how much Levi belongs to God. I was trying to imagine if God could possibly love him more than I do. In my own mind and heart, I can love Levi no deeper. I love him entirely, consumingly. He was God's first. I think I love Levi because he was our creation, in a sense. He was Roy's and mine. But he was God's creation first. It's almost as if there is no belonging in this world. The soul is the thing that lives and belongs.

Levi's headstone reads, "Born into the Presence of God." That is a wonderful reality.

November 1987

Monday, November 2

We went into the city yesterday. I dropped Roy off at the gravesite so he could lay Levi's tombstone while I went to visit the family. When I came to pick him up, he was sitting on a nearby gravestone looking at Levi's. That was a hard time for my honey. Through sobs and tears he said, "It looks nice doesn't it?" Hard times to lay the gravestone of your firstborn son. God grant us another one. No. Just grant us yourself. You are our all in all. We know that now. As Job said,

> *"My ears had heard of you but now
> my eyes have seen you."*
> Job 42:5 (NIV)

Just grant us Yourself. Just grant us Yourself. You ARE the words of Life.

Tuesday, November 3

Okay, I have so much to write down. I'm so busy with my production class I hardly have time to journal. Life can change in an instant. It looks like our next child might come through adoption! Just a minute, Lord. Slow down. No, don't slow down, but

I need to think. Can't give my heart away yet. There are so many scary variables.

So, here's what happened: I was having tea with Gloria ...

But that's another story.

Epilogue:

Our children did indeed come to us through adoption. I had one miscarriage (we named this baby Christian Hope) between our two adopted children. Some years later, I discovered I had severe endometriosis, which often causes infertility. I have no doubt that God's Plan A was exactly what happened for our family. Megan was adopted at birth, in 1988, one and one-half years after Levi was born; Bronwyn came to us in 1991, at birth, three and one-half years later. I always tell our children that God had planned before time began for them to be "Bennett girls." They are our covenant children and we are all thankful for God's goodness in choosing us for each other. We often say to one another, "I'm so glad that you are mine." Levi Nielsen and Christian Hope are a part of our family. We know that "this world is not our home, we're just passing through." Heaven is precious, but then…so is grief.

Barry and Maine went on to have two daughters (the very same ages as our girls) both of whom were born with Cystic Fibrosis. Yes, our stories are not all the same. But everyone has a story…

"In the beginning was the Word…In him was life…"
John 1:1a & 4a
"Lord, to whom shall we go? You
have the words of eternal life."
John 6:68b
Be silent and know that He is God.

The End.

About the Author:

Norma Bennett lives in California, with the same Karachi sandal-wearing husband. Her life has been full of words, both spoken and written. For more information about her work go to: bennett-projects.com

71049612R00041

Made in the USA
San Bernardino, CA
12 March 2018